D1547196

MARRYING THE ROSARY
TO THE
DIVINE MERCY CHAPLET

MARRYING THE ROSARY
TO THE
DIVINE MERCY CHAPLET

A free gift!

Download an audio companion at:
http://tinyurl.com/kapler

SHANE KAPLER

© En Route Books & Media, 2016
5705 Rhodes Avenue, St. Louis, MO 63109
Contact us at contactus@enroutebooksandmedia.com
Find En Route online at www.enroutebooksandmedia.com

Cover design by TJ Burdick, cover image credits:

Adolf Hyla, Kraków Divine Mercy Image, 1938 via wikimediea: https://upload.wikimedia.org/wikipedia/commons/thumb/c/c9/ Jes%C3%BAs_en_Vos_conf%C3%ADo.jpg/707px-Jes%C3%BAs_ en_Vos_conf%C3%ADo.jpg

Texture: Public Domain Pictures, Edited: http://www. publicdomainpictures.net/pictures/90000/nahled/red-texture-1399555232jNI.jpg

Hanging Rosary—gracey, via morguefile.com: http://morguefile.com/ search/morguefile/2/rosary/pop

Silhouette of the Virgin and child—OpenClipart Vectors—via pixabay: https://pixabay.com/p-1294124/?no_redirect

Silhouette of Jesus on the cross—jingoba via pixabay- https://pixabay. com/p-404147/?no_redirect

Hardback ISBN: 978-1-63337-149-1
Paperback ISBN: 978-1-63337-150-7
E-book ISBN: 978-1-63337-151-4
LCCN: 2016960342

Printed in the United States of America

CONTENTS

THE SORROWFUL MYSTERIES

THE GLORIOUS MYSTERIES

This book is dedicated to:
My daily prayer partners, my children,
Lily and Brennan
and
Annie Mitchell Egan,
whose enthusiasm inspired me to put these thoughts on paper

FOREWORD

For more than 800 years, the Rosary has been used by the Church as a spiritual weapon and way of crowning Our Lady with heavenly roses. The Rosary has overcome the enemies of Christ, saved entire nations, stopped wars, and helped many lost souls find their way back to the practice of the faith and the Sacraments.

In the early 20th century, when Jesus revealed the Chaplet of the Divine Mercy to Saint Faustina, he desired that ordinary rosary beads be used as the material component for a new form of devotion to his mercy. This moment, in a certain sense, marks the "engagement" of the Rosary to the Chaplet. Everyone knows that marriages take time, planning, and preparation. This marriage, in particular, has been long in the making. It is truly a marriage made in heaven.

In the 13th century, when Our Lady gave the Rosary to Saint Dominic, the Founder of the Dominicans never would have imagined that centuries later the world would be in such moral decline that heaven would wed to the blessed battle beads of St. Dominic a new form of devotion to God's mercy. The revelations of Jesus to Saint Faustina would give the Rosary the added power of not only being a spiritual weapon and a heavenly crown of roses, but also an instrument of mercy for a hurting world. Jesus knows that Divine Mercy is exactly what our world needs today.

In this devotional marriage, then, Saint Faustina Kowalska serves as the bride's maid and Saint John Paul II the best man. Both of these great saints prayed the Rosary every day and were apostles of the Divine Mercy message and devotion. I am quite certain they would both be very pleased to witness the marriage of the Rosary to the Chaplet as presented in this book.

The method of prayer presented by Shane Kapler in this book has the potential to produce an abundance of fruit in the spiritual lives of those who use it. After all, all marriages are called to fruitfulness. By using this method of prayer, people will be able to meditate on the saving mysteries of Jesus and, at the same time, make an urgent appeal to God's mercy for ourselves and the whole world. What better union could there be? What incredible fruit will come from this form of devotion!

Saint Dominic, pray for us!   Saint Faustina, pray for us! Saint John Paul II, pray for us!

Fr. Donald Calloway, MIC, STL
Author of *Champions of the Rosary:*
The History and Heroes of a Spiritual Weapon

INTRODUCTION

I cannot think of two more popular devotions than the Rosary and the Chaplet of Divine Mercy. That isn't surprising, though, given the way that Heaven has intervened so dramatically to bring them to our attention. In 1917, the Blessed Mother came to Fatima, Portugal to request the daily praying of the Rosary; and in 1935, our Lord revealed the Chaplet of Divine Mercy to St. Faustina Kowalska and requested that she make it known. In this small booklet you will discover how uniting these two devotions – how interspersing the decades of the Rosary with the Chaplet – is a powerful way to deepen the meditation and intercession proper to both.

TWO POWERFUL, COMPLEMENTARY DEVOTIONS

The Church, of course, does not require us to acquiesce to private revelations such as those to the children of Fatima or

St. Faustina. And yet, even if we set private revelation aside, the theological profundity of these two devotions is more than evident. The Rosary highlights the communion of saints and our need to meditate upon Scripture; and the Chaplet is a living proclamation of the Gospel – that all graces flow to us as a result of Christ's Passion.

In the Rosary we contemplate Jesus through the eyes of his mother. The Apostles spent the nine days between Jesus' ascension and Pentecost with Mary, meditating on her Son's life in the light of Scripture (Acts 1:14, 20). *We do the same when we pray the Rosary.* We join Mary in prayer, invoking her intercession in the words of Scripture – the Hail Mary (Lk. 1:28, 42). That intentionally repeated invocation acts as a sacred "soundtrack" as our hearts and minds ponder Jesus' words and actions in the four gospels and Acts of the Apostles. We begin each period of meditation praying the Our Father, the prayer of Christ (Mt. 6:9-13; CCC 2765), and we conclude by praising God in the words of Christ and his angels, "Glory be to…" (Lk. 2:14; Mt. 28:19; Rev. 1:8).

In the Chaplet we do spiritually what in the Eucharist we do sacramentally – unite our individual prayers to the infallible intercession of Christ Crucified. The gift Jesus made of himself on the Cross superabundantly atoned for humanity's sins and opened the floodgates of God's sanctifying grace. In the Chaplet we ask the Father to pour out his mercy; and St. Thomas Aquinas reminds us that mercy is more than pardoning sin (as necessary as that is) – it also means to supply what another is lacking (*ST* II-II.30.1). The chaplet petitions the Father to forgive our sins and pour out the grace and virtues we lack – *because of what Jesus did at the Cross.* We mentally immerse ourselves in Christ's Passion as we offer the Father the body, blood, soul, and divinity of his dearly beloved Son.

Both the Rosary and Chaplet provide a meditative entry into the life of Christ, and both are prayers of intercession. In the Rosary, meditation is to the fore; whereas in the Chaplet it is intercession. Each is beautiful and sufficient in and of itself, and I continue to regularly pray each separately. In the pages that follow, however, I share the synergy I discovered by following a decade of the Rosary with a decade of the Chaplet.

DEVOTIONAL NUTS AND BOLTS

If you have rosary beads – or really any means of counting to ten (yes, fingers will do) – then you have the physical aspect covered. Since the Rosary's introductory prayers are mirrored in the Chaplet, you will start by praying the Rosary as usual: Begin by making the Sign of the Cross, the Gospel in miniature. Recall how Christ's Cross has introduced you into the inner life of the Father, Son, and Spirit; and how God's merciful grace empowers you to fulfill the Great Commandment to love the Lord our God with all our mind (touch your forehead), all our heart (heart), and all our strength (both shoulders). Then proceed to pray the Apostles' Creed, making each of its tenets an exclamation of the heart as you bless God for the gift of your faith. Continue by joining yourself to the Lord Jesus, as you pray the Our Father. Then approach our Blessed Mother. As you pray the three Hail Marys, ask her to intercede that the Lord will give you her heart with which to serve him, that you will share in *her* faith, hope, and charity. Conclude the introductory prayers by praising God with the Glory Be.

It is now time to begin your meditation on the first mystery of the Rosary. Begin with the Our Father and then pray ten Hail Marys aloud as you interiorly ponder the mystery. When you come to the end of the decade, pray the Glory Be and the Fatima Prayer, "O my Jesus, forgive us our sins. Save us from the fires of hell. Lead all souls to heaven, especially those in most need of thy mercy." Then pray one decade of the Chaplet:

On the Our Father bead: Eternal Father, I offer You the Body and Blood, Soul and Divinity of Your dearly beloved Son, Our Lord Jesus Christ, in atonement for our sins and those of the whole world.

On the ten Hail Mary beads: For the sake of His sorrowful Passion have mercy on us and on the whole world.

Repeat this pattern for the four remaining Rosary mysteries, and conclude your prayer with the triple recitation of the Trisagion[1] and the Hail Holy Queen.

---

1   "Holy God, Holy, Mighty One, Holy Immortal One, have mercy on us and on the whole world."

BENEFITS

When I combined my praying of the Rosary with the Chaplet, my rosary meditation was led in unexpected directions. In the Joyful and Luminous Mysteries I discovered anew a truth articulated by Ven. Fulton J. Sheen: The Cross cast its shadow backward over our Lord's entire life. In the Sorrowful Mysteries I found my awareness of Jesus' pain deepened; and in the Glorious I found our Catholic conviction that the Cross is the precondition of glory – both in Christ's earthly journey and in our own –powerfully affirmed. But that was not all.

I also realized that when I brought the Chaplet into the Rosary, I invited Mary to pray the Chaplet with me. We stood together at the foot of the Cross, the Chaplet allowing me to voice her prayer, "Eternal Father, I offer you…" Together we joined ourselves to Jesus' offering and, through it, interceded that the fruits of his sacrifice to be generously poured out upon the Church and world.

HOW TO USE THIS BOOK

This book has been arranged according to the Rosary's four sets of mysteries. Many people follow the tradition of praying the Joyful Mysteries on Mondays and Saturdays, the Luminous on Thursdays, Sorrowful on Tuesdays and Fridays, and the Glorious on Wednesdays and Sundays.

At the beginning of each reflection you will find the title of the mystery and a scriptural reference. If you have not studied the Bible before, then I strongly recommend that you read these short passages. In all honesty, though, reading is of benefit to even the most seasoned biblical scholar. In Scripture we have the mysteries of the Rosary narrated in the *very words of God* (*Dei Verbum*, 11)! No matter how well we think we know the events, no matter how many times we may have read the passages before, Scripture is not just human but *divine* – and therefore, an inexhaustible source of insights. As questions arise in your reading address them directly to the Holy Spirit and continue to ponder, to meditate upon, what you have read about this mystery.

The meat of each page is devoted to helping you with your meditation. Before you begin your vocal prayer, slowly read the provided reflection. These are thoughts, connections, that occurred to me during my own praying of the mystery. As I have said, anticipation of praying a decade of the Chaplet colored my reflection, showing the Cross's connection to all that came before and after. You may want to open your Bible to check the additional Scriptural references provided in the body of the meditation. As you move from the Our Father to the praying of the Hail Marys, consider what you have read. Allow your mind to follow any new connections that arise.

Finally, let your period of meditation focus your praying of the Chaplet. Petition God for the mercy, the grace, to live what you have seen in the lives of Jesus and Mary. I have provided the petitions and intercessions that arose in my own prayer. In the Rosary we gazed upon Jesus with the eyes of Mary; we now invite her to join us in petitioning God for the mercies we seek.

By praying the Rosary and Chaplet in this way, you will practice the first three steps of *lectio divina*, or divine reading. Scripture is read, meditated upon, and then God is addressed in prayer. The final step of *lectio divina*, contemplation, we confide to the Holy Spirit. In the Rosary and Chaplet we cooperate with the Spirit in breaking up the fallowed ground of our hearts and seeding and watering them with the Word of God. We entrust the growth of the divine life within us and the resultant experience of union with God to the Spirit. Now, let us begin.

THE JOYFUL MYSTERIES

Joy in the Shadow of the Cross

The Annunciation, Henry Osawa Tanner, 1898

THE ANNUNCIATION

(LUKE 1:26-38)

Mary recognized herself as the Lord's handmaid (*doulē* in Greek, "slave"). St. Paul applied the term, in its masculine form, to Jesus, who "though he was in the form of God, did not count equality with God a thing to be grasped, but emptied himself, taking the form of a slave (*doulou*), being born in the likeness of men (Phil. 2:6-7). The "slavery" borne by Jesus and Mary was not one of exterior coercion, but love. They loved the Father so intensely that their deepest human desire was for union with him. That love impelled them to embrace the divine will that the Son become man and give his life upon the Cross (Heb. 10:5-7).

It was through the *eternal Spirit* that Jesus offered himself to the Father (Heb. 9:14). It was the same Spirit who "overshadowed" Mary and empowered her to give her "yes," to the Incarnation. She participated in the "yes" of the Son. Just as Jesus's "not my will, but thine, be done" in Gethsemane led to his arms being stretched out on Calvary, so Mary's "let it be to me according to your word" caused her body and soul to be stretched as Christ grew within her.

Mary was able to make this complete gift herself because she had been prepared for it since her conception. Gabriel addressed her as *Kecharitomene*, the one who has been, and is now, completely filled with God's grace. Jesus was the Lamb slain from the foundation of the world (Rev. 13:8), and by the merits of his sorrowful Passion, Mary was preserved free from the stain of original sin. In God's tremendous mercy she was saved by Christ in the most complete manner possible.

Decade of the Rosary: Our Father, ten Hail Marys, Glory Be, Fatima Prayer

Pray: Dear Jesus, standing with your mother at the foot of your Cross and filled with your Spirit, we pray...

Chaplet Intercession: Father, remove any barriers we have erected to the operation of grace in our lives. Let your Holy Spirit overshadow us and form Christ in the womb of our hearts. Give us the grace to embrace your will with every fiber of our being.

Decade of the Chaplet: "Eternal Father...," ten "For the sake..."

Adolf Hyla, *Kraków Divine Mercy Image*, 1938

Domenico Ghirlandaio,
*Mary, pregnant with Jesus, visits her elderly cousin Elizabeth,
pregnant with John the Baptist,* c. 1491

THE VISITATION

(LUKE 1:39-56)

Elizabeth lived in the hill country of Judea, on the out-skirts of Jerusalem. Did Mary's travel take her within view of any of the criminals crucified outside the city walls? How close did she pass to Golgotha?

From within Mary's womb, Jesus bestows the Holy Spirit upon John and his mother. Like David before the Ark of God, John leaps in the presence of Mary and Jesus (Lk. 1:43-44; 2 Sam. 6:9-16). Both children would give their lives – Jesus in propitiation for our sins, and John for calling the powers-that-be to honor God's vision of marriage.

When Elizabeth blesses Mary, Mary directs the praise to the God who lavished his grace upon her. In her song of praise, her *Magnificat*, she speaks words that make our hearts leap, "his mercy is on those who fear him from generation to gener-ation" (Lk. 1:50). God's mercy is offered freely, but it was not cheap. We were ransomed "not with perishable things such as silver or gold, but with the precious blood of Christ" (1 Pet.

1:18-19). We no longer belong to ourselves but, like Mary, to God, and we have a duty to honor his presence within us by living lives of holiness (1 Cor. 6:19-20).

Mary's *Magnificat* also speaks to us of the perfect union between God's mercy and his justice. The Father disciplines us so that we can give birth to Jesus in our lives. He pulls the mighty off their thrones so that they can become the humble whom he will later exult. He sends the rich away empty so that they will return hungry for the Bread of Life.

Decade of the Rosary: Our Father, ten Hail Marys, Glory Be, Fatima Prayer

Pray: Dear Jesus, standing with your mother at the foot of your Cross and filled with your Spirit, we pray…

Chaplet Intercession: Father, give us the grace to recognize your fatherly discipline for the mercy that it truly is. Fill us anew with your Spirit so that, united with Mary in the mystical body of your Son, we may carry Jesus to our family, friends, and co-workers.

Decade of the Chaplet: "Eternal Father…," ten "For the sake…"

The Return of the Prodigal Son,
Bartolomé Esteban Murillo, 1667-1670

The Adoration of the Shepherds,
Gerard van Honthorst, 1622

THE NATIVITY

(LUKE 2:1-20)

The Nativity draws our attention to the symmetry of God's redemptive plan. Mary gives birth to Jesus in Bethlehem ("House of Bread" in Hebrew) and lays Him in a manger, a feeding trough for animals. It prefigures the Eucharist, the memorial of his Paschal mystery.

The cave of the Nativity points ahead to the cave in which Jesus was buried...and raised. The angels tell the shepherds, "this will be a *sign* for you: you will find a baby wrapped in swaddling cloths and lying in a manger" (Lk. 2:12). Decades later the Apostle John will gaze into Christ's tomb and, seeing "the linen cloths lying there" by themselves, come to faith in the Resurrection (John 20:4-9). For both John and the shepherds the wrappings acted as a sign. For the shepherds it was Jesus' presence in the bands; but for John, his absence.

At Christ's birth the angelic host proclaims, "Glory to God in the highest, and on earth *peace* among men with whom he is pleased!" (Lk. 2:14). That peace was fully bestowed after

22

our Lord's Passion, on the evening of the Resurrection, "Peace be with you" (John 20:19). And if we should lose that peace through grave sin, Christ gave the apostles the sacrament of reconciliation to restore it to us, "Jesus said to them again, 'Peace be with you...If you forgive the sins of any, they are forgiven; if you retain the sins of any, they are retained" (John 20:21-23).

Decade of the Rosary: Our Father, ten Hail Marys, Glory Be, Fatima Prayer

Pray: Dear Jesus, standing with your mother at the foot of your Cross and filled with your Spirit, we pray...

Chaplet Intercession: Father we ask your mercy for all those have not yet come to faith; let them see in Christ's Cross the ultimate sign of your love. For those who believe, but keep their distance because of sin, give them the grace to receive your mercy in the sacrament of reconciliation.

Decade of the Chaplet: "Eternal Father...," ten "For the sake..."

St. John and St. Peter at Christ's Tomb,
Giovanni Francesco Romanelli, 1640

Presentation at the temple, Hans Holbein the Elder,
1500-1501

THE PRESENTATION

(LUKE 2:22-38)

There in the arms of his mother, Simeon sees the small face he has waited a lifetime to gaze upon. Simeon embraces the child, and his heart erupts with joy as he praises God for the salvation that Christ will bring – not just to Israel, but the world. Simeon's face turns grave, however, as his soul begins to perceive the manner in which Jesus will achieve our salvation. Looking from Jesus to Mary's gentle face, Simeon knows that the Passion of the Son will be the passion of the mother. "[A]nd a sword will pierce through your own soul also, that thoughts out of many hearts may be revealed" (Lk. 2:35). Mary is called to renew her "yes" to God's will. As Simeon places Jesus back into the arms of His mother, we glimpse the *Pieta*.

Decades later the Holy Spirit inspired St. Paul to write to the Colossians, "I rejoice in my sufferings for your sake, and in my flesh I complete what is lacking in Christ's afflictions for the sake of his body, that is, the Church" (Col. 1:24). Paul's suffered because of his union with Christ, but the Lord

Jesus made that suffering fruitful for Paul's soul and the souls of countless others. And if that was true of Paul, then how much more so of Mary? No one was united to Jesus more profoundly, suffered more deeply, or has been more spiritually fruitful than our Blessed Mother.

Decade of the Rosary: Our Father, ten Hail Marys, Glory Be, Fatima Prayer

Pray: Dear Jesus, standing with your mother at the foot of your Cross and filled with your Spirit, we pray…

Chaplet Intercession: Father, like Jesus, we are signs of contradiction in this fallen world. We ask for the grace to persevere when persecuted. Please give us the grace to stand beside Mary – as Joseph did in the Temple, and as John did on Good Friday – and share whatever portion of Jesus' Passion you have allotted us. Make our suffering redemptive.

Decade of the Chaplet: "Eternal Father…," ten "For the sake…"

Pietà, William-Adolphe Bouguereau, 1876

Jesus Among the Doctors, Giotto di Bondone, 1303-1305

THE FINDING IN THE TEMPLE

(LUKE 2:41-51)

Mary's heart pulsed with joy at the sight of her Son, but only after she had searched for him for three frantic, *agonizing* days. Any parent who has ever turned around in a store and experienced the rush of terror at not seeing his or her child, can enter into Mary's pain. For her, though, it was but a foretaste of the three days when she would lose Jesus to the grave.

Jesus expressed surprise that Mary and Joseph needed to search for him, "Did you not know that I must be in my Father's house?" (Lk. 2:49). The Lord repeats that question to you and me. Whenever we feel lost or at a distance from God, Jesus reminds us that He is as close as the nearest parish church. He is fully present to us there in the tabernacle – body, blood, soul, and divinity. He awaits us as a patient lover. May we share Mary's joy at finding him there.

The Gospel says that Jesus went home and was obedient to Mary and Joseph. He did so, ultimately out of love for, and obedience to, the Father. Christ's obedience extended all the way to the Cross, where he subjected himself to the judgment of Pilate (Jn. 19:11; Heb. 5:8). Whenever we submit to the authority of those that God has placed over us in the Church – the pope and bishops - we participate in the human obedience of Christ. We manifest the submission that God the Son made to a poor carpenter and a young maiden (and even to a weak-willed, pagan governor) out of obedience to the Father.

Decade of the Rosary: Our Father, ten Hail Marys, Glory Be, Fatima Prayer

Pray: Dear Jesus, standing with your mother at the foot of your Cross and filled with your Spirit, we pray…

Chaplet Intercession: Father, give us a longing for Jesus in the Eucharist – a longing to sit in his Eucharistic presence, a longing to receive him into ourselves; and in doing so, give us the strength to fully submit ourselves to your will.

Decade of the Chaplet: "Eternal Father…," ten "For the sake…"

Triple Recitation of the Trisagion ("Holy God, Holy Mighty…"); *conclude with Hail Holy Queen*

Disputation of the Sacrament, Raphael, 1509-1510

THE LUMINOUS MYSTERIES

Christ's Light and the Shadow of the Cross

Baptism of Christ Fresco, Pietro Perugino, 1482

Jesus' Baptism in the Jordan River

(Mark 1:9-13)

"You are my beloved Son; with you I am well pleased" (Mk.1:11). The Father's simple declaration is rich in meaning. The Father addresses Jesus by bringing together verses of Scripture written hundreds of years apart, Psalm 2:7 and Isaiah 42:1. The first was addressed to the coming Messiah, and the second to God's mysteriously prophesied "Servant," who would be "bruised for our iniquities" and bear "the chastisement that made us whole" (Is. 53:5).

When Jesus went down into the waters of the Jordan, he publicly assumed his role as the suffering Messiah. John the Baptist recognized him as the Lamb of God (Jn. 1:36; Is. 53:6-7). Jesus, the sinless one, took upon himself our need to repent. It was as our representative that he received John's baptism of *repentance* (Mt. 3:11). The chill of the Jordan bespoke the chill of death that would encompass him on the Cross.

The power of the Spirit then "drove" Jesus into the desert to relive and redeem Israel's forty years of wandering and Adam's surrender to temptation. For forty days Jesus denied himself food and companionship, making reparation for the ways we misuse these gifts, and he emerged victorious as the one infinitely stronger than sin and Satan (Lk. 11:20-22).

Decade of the Rosary: Our Father, ten Hail Marys, Glory Be, Fatima Prayer

Pray: Dear Jesus, standing with your mother at the foot of your Cross and filled with your Spirit, we pray...

Chaplet Intercession: Father, *move our hearts* to renounce whatever is not of you. Have mercy and, through your Spirit, set us free from our inordinate attachments and addictions.

Decade of the Chaplet: "Eternal Father...," ten "For the sake..."

Temptation on the Mount, Duccio di Buoninsegna,
between 1308 and 1311

The Wedding at Cana, Paolo Veronese, 1563

THE WEDDING FEAST OF CANA

(JOHN 2:1-11)

Jesus' response when approached by the Blessed Mother about the shortage of wine is jarring. "Woman, how does your concern affect me? My hour has not yet come" (Jn. 2:4, NAB). His *hour*? The remainder of John's Gospel makes clear that Jesus' hour refers to his Passion and death (Jn. 16:32; 17:1). Jesus went on to grant Mary's request, making it the first of his *signs* (Jn. 2:11). Jesus' changing of the water into wine was a sign that pointed ahead to his hour, to his sacrificial passage from this world to the Father and the new age it inaugurated. It pointed ahead to the *definitive* wedding feast and the wine for which every human heart thirsts.

Centuries before our Lord's birth Isaiah had prophesied how, in the Messianic Age, God would provide all the peoples of the world with a "feast of rich food and choice wines" (Is. 25:6). It was on the Cross that the Grape (Christ's body) was crushed, and the New Wine (his blood) flowed; and it is in the Eucharist – the wedding feast of the Lamb (Rev. 19:7-9) – that they are given to us as supernatural food and drink.

40

Decade of the Rosary: Our Father, ten Hail Marys, Glory Be, Fatima Prayer

Pray: Dear Jesus, standing with your mother at the foot of your Cross and filled with your Spirit, we pray…

Chaplet Intercession: Father, bring our loved ones who have fallen away back to the celebration of the Eucharist. Bring back *all* who have fallen away. Show them their spiritual hunger and move their hearts to return.

Decade of the Chaplet: "Eternal Father…," ten "For the sake…"

Mystical Winepress, Albrecht Dürer's workshop,
1510 approx

Sermon on the Mount by Cosimo Rosselli, 1481-1482

THE PROCLAMATION OF THE KINGDOM

(MATTHEW 4:17-25)

Walking beside the Sea of Galilee, Jesus called Peter, Andrew, James, and John to leave their fishing business to follow him and become "fishers of men" (Mt. 4:19). Their response exemplifies discipleship: They "immediately" dropped their nets and spent the next three years assisting Jesus in his proclamation of the Kingdom. They were at his side as he mesmerized the crowds with is words, healed the sick, and expelled demons with a simple command.

Where were these four exemplary apostles, though, when Jesus was crucified? Only John had the courage to stand before the Lord's Cross (Jn. 19:26). In Jesus' greatest hour of need Peter, Andrew, and James hid in fear. Peter denied even knowing him! Scripture warns us, "[W]hoever thinks he is standing secure should take care not to fall" (1 Cor. 10:12, NAB). There are many ways that we can deny the Lord – being ashamed of his teaching (Mark 8:38), refusing to care for him in the needy (Matt. 25:31-46), rejecting those he entrusts with his word (Luke 10:16).

Decade of the Rosary: Our Father, ten Hail Marys, Glory Be, Fatima Prayer

Pray: Dear Jesus, standing with your mother at the foot of your Cross and filled with your Spirit, we pray…"

Chaplet Intercession: Father, give us the grace of final perseverance that we may leave this world intimately united to you.

Decade of the Chaplet: "Eternal Father…," ten "For the sake…"

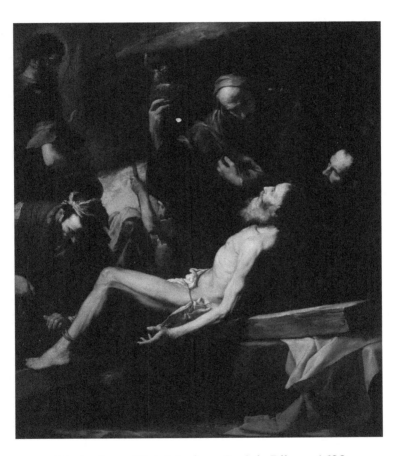

Martyrdom of Saint Andrew, José de Ribera, 1628

The Transfiguration, Raphael, 1516-1520

THE TRANSFIGURATION

(LUKE 9:28-36)

The apostles witnessed Moses and Elijah speaking with Jesus about his "exodus," his Passover from this world to the Father (Lk. 9:31). They heard the Father speak from the cloud of glory, "This is my *beloved Son*. Listen to him" (Mk. 9:7). It takes our minds to another mountain, the one scaled by Abraham and his beloved son, Isaac (Gen. 22:2). Isaac climbed, carrying the wood of sacrifice on his shoulders. Abraham intuited that God would send a lamb to take his son's place upon the altar (Gen. 22:8). It was a *type*, an image, of the Passover which, in turn, was a type of Christ's sacrifice and the Eucharist.

Our Lord's transfiguration foreshadowed his Resurrection. Before the apostles beheld Jesus transfigured in glory, however, they had to climb a mountain. There is no Resurrection without the preliminary experience of the Cross. "[I]f we have been united with him in a death like his, we shall certainly be united with him in a resurrection like his" (Rom. 6:5).

Decade of the Rosary: Our Father, ten Hail Marys, Glory Be, Fatima Prayer

Pray: Dear Jesus, standing with your mother at the foot of your Cross and filled with your Spirit, we pray…

Chaplet Intercession: Father, give us the grace to embrace your Son's Cross.

Decade of the Chaplet: "Eternal Father…," ten "For the sake…"

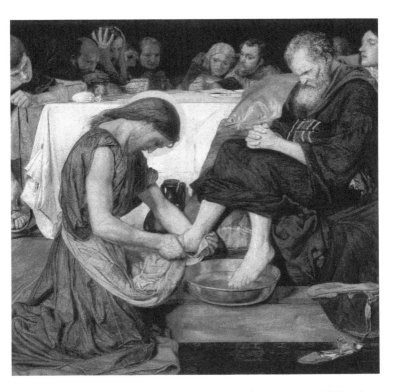

Jesus Washing Peter's Feet, Ford Madox Brown, 1852–6

The Last Supper, Juan de Juanes, 1560

THE INSTITUTION OF THE EUCHARIST

(LUKE 22:14-20)

"I have *eagerly desired* to eat this Passover with you before I suffer" (Lk. 22:15). Who but our Lord could speak that way in the face of death? Jesus' love for us is truly unfathomable.

"This is my body...This cup is the new covenant in my blood...do this *in memory* of me" (Lk. 22:19-20). "In memory" – *zikkaron* in Hebrew, is not a memory exercise, but a cultic act that makes a past event *present*. At his final Passover meal, when he instituted the Eucharist, Jesus made his sacrifice present by anticipation and joined the apostles to it. His sacrifice, the act of a divine Person, is present to all of history (Heb. 9:14). Jesus is the Lamb slain "from the foundation of the world" (Rev. 13:8). His offering becomes present to us in the Eucharist; and we must constantly make use of it to come boldly to "the throne of grace, that we may receive mercy and find grace to help in time of need" (Heb. 4:16).

Decade of the Rosary: Our Father, ten Hail Marys, Glory Be, Fatima Prayer

Pray: Dear Jesus, standing with your mother at the foot of your Cross and filled with your Spirit, we pray…

Chaplet Intercession: Father, open our eyes anew to the depths of your Son's love for us. Let us enter wholeheartedly into his Eucharistic sacrifice, worshiping you with body and soul.

Decade of the Chaplet: "Eternal Father…," ten "For the sake…"

Triple Recitation of the Trisagion ("Holy God, Holy Mighty…"); *conclude with Hail Holy Queen*

The Last Supper, Carl Heinrich Bloch, late 19th century

THE SORROWFUL MYSTERIES

THE CROSS REALIZED

Agony in the Garden, Orazio Borgianni, 1610

THE AGONY IN THE GARDEN

(LUKE 22:39-46)

We see Jesus as we have never seen him before: collapsed on the ground, repeatedly petitioning the Father with loud cries and tears that, if possible, the cup of suffering would be removed (Mk. 14:35; Heb. 5:7). His closest friends provide no support – with their stomachs full from the Passover feast, they drift off to sleep, blissfully unaware of the storm about to break upon them. Amidst this all, our Lord's heart is resolute, "nevertheless not my will, but yours, be done" (Lk. 22:42). We make his petition our own in the Our Father.

As our savior, Jesus stands in our place, the place of sinners. "[T]he LORD has laid on him the iniquity of us all" (Is. 53:6). His human soul beholds every act of evil – every betrayal, deception, slander, rape, murder – from history's dawn until its consummation; and from the depths of his sacred heart, he pours forth to the Father all of the sorrow and contrition that *we should feel* for our sins, but do not. Jesus will love and obey the Father in the midst of the most excruciating physical and spiritual suffering imaginable, *in atonement for our sins*.

Blood is in Jesus' sweat – *hematidrosis*, a result of the excruciating anxiety He is experiencing. The sins of all men and women are more than one human nature can endure. In his great humility, Jesus receives an infusion of strength not directly from his divine nature, but through the intermediary of an angel, a creature. This infusion allows him to endure more than humanly possible. Instead of expiring in the garden, he will live to endure the Passion in all its physical brutality.

Decade of the Rosary: Our Father, ten Hail Marys, Glory Be, Fatima Prayer

Pray: Dear Jesus, standing with your mother at the foot of your Cross and filled with your Spirit, we pray…

Chaplet Intercession: Father, imbue those of us who dread what tomorrow will bring with Christ's strength. In the midst of anxiety, move our hearts to say, "not my will, but thy will be done."

Decade of the Chaplet: "Eternal Father…," ten "For the sake…"

Christ before Caiaphas, Matthias Stom, early 1630s

Flagellation of Christ, Peter Paul Rubens, c. 1617

THE SCOURGING AT THE PILLAR

(MARK 15:12-15)

The effects of our Lord's Passion are cumulative. The sweating of blood in Gethsemane has left his skin particularly sensitive. The soldiers have stripped him naked and fastened his hands to the top of the pillar. The Roman whip was an instrument of brutality; metal barbs at the tip cut into Jesus' muscles and rip away ribbons of flesh. His back is one gaping wound. "With his stripes we are healed" (Is. 53:5).

The Church shares her Lord's Passion. Jesus told the apostles that they too would be flogged (Mt. 10:17). Paul alone suffered five floggings (2 Cor. 11:24)! Such knowledge frightens us. We must allow our souls to be naked before the Lord, acknowledging our fear of suffering for Him.

Decade of the Rosary: Our Father, ten Hail Marys, Glory Be, Fatima Prayer

Pray: Dear Jesus, standing with your mother at the foot of your

Cross and filled with your Spirit, we pray...

Chaplet Intercession: Father, we acknowledge our fear of pain and ask for the grace to keep moving forward as disciples nonetheless.

Decade of the Chaplet: "Eternal Father...," ten "For the sake..."

The Flagellation of Our Lord Jesus Christ,
William-Adolphe Bouguereau, 1880

The Crown of Thorns, Anthony van Dyck, c. 1620

THE CROWNING WITH THORNS

(MATTHEW 27:27-30)

Our Lord's back is one gaping wound, so the pain receptors are triggered anew when the soldiers drape the rough, scarlet cloak over his shoulders. Each time you and I sin we make a vain ploy to usurp God's role as King. We place a false crown upon our heads and justly deserve to be mocked. Jesus stands in the place of sinners, taking a crown of thorns upon himself. He, the God-Man who deserves to wear the most ornate crown imaginable, chooses instead to wear our crown of shame. "[U]pon him was the chastisement that made us whole" (Is. 53:5).

Our Lord's world must have turned red as the blood flowed down his forehead and into his eyes. He feels each blow of the reed as the soldiers repeatedly strike his skull, driving the thorns deeper.

Decade of the Rosary: Our Father, ten Hail Marys, Glory Be, Fatima Prayer

Pray: Dear Jesus, standing with your mother at the foot of your Cross and filled with your Spirit, we pray…

Chaplet Intercession: Father, forgive us. Remove us from the "thrones" of our lives, and let Jesus assume his rightful place there.

Decade of the Chaplet: "Eternal Father…," ten "For the sake…"

St Jerome, Titian, between 1570 and 1575

Christ Carrying the Cross, Giorgio Vasari, c. 1562–1565

THE CARRYING
OF THE CROSS

(MATTHEW 27:31-32)

The wounds on Jesus' back can be seen bleeding through his garment as the soldiers place the horizontal beam of the Cross, the *patibulum*, on his shoulders. As the soldiers lash his hands to the beam, its one hundred pounds sink into Jesus' flayed shoulders. His head is pounding and his heart racing as he begins the march to Calvary. "Surely he has borne our griefs and carried our sorrows" (Is. 53:4).

Weak from the beatings and loss of blood, Jesus falls. His hands are tied so there is no way to break his fall; the Cross drives his face into the stone ground. The soldiers, not wanting Jesus to expire on the march, pull Simon of Cyrene from the crowd and force him to carry the Cross behind Jesus.

We want to be other Simons, making our Lord's weight easier to bear - *and we can*. "Truly, I say to you, as you did it to one of the least of these my brethren, you did it to me" (Mt. 25:40). We see the hurt and struggle in people's lives, and the sheer magnitude makes us want to run the other way; but St.

Paul tells us to, "Bear one another's burdens, and so fulfil the law of Christ" (Gal. 6:2). At the Last Supper, Jesus said, "A new commandment I give to you, that you love one another; *even as I have loved you*" (John 13:34). In his great, merciful love for us, Christ took the Cross upon his shoulders. We extend that merciful love to others when we take their crosses upon ours.

Decade of the Rosary: Our Father, ten Hail Marys, Glory Be, Fatima Prayer

Pray: Dear Jesus, standing with your mother at the foot of your Cross and filled with your Spirit, we pray…

Chaplet Intercession: Father, give us the grace to enter into other people's struggles and the wisdom to know how to truly be of service to them.

Decade of the Chaplet: "Eternal Father…," ten "For the sake…"

Christ Carrying the Cross, Titian, 1565

Crucifixion, Matthias Grunewald, 1523-1525

THE CRUCIFIXION

(LUKE 23:33-46)

Our Lord is laid in the dirt, his hands placed on the wood, and spikes driven through his wrists. Jesus' pain is unimaginable as the *patibulum* is lifted up and attached to the horizontal beam of the Cross. Spikes are then driven through his feet. Passersby deride him, "If you are the Son of God, come down from the cross" (Mt. 27:40). He proves his love for us by remaining where he is.

He hangs there, suffocating under his own weight. To take a breath he must push down on his pierced feet, pull up on the spikes passing through His wrists, and drag His mangled back over the Cross's harsh wood. Even so, Jesus pulls himself up to capture enough breath to speak:

"Father, forgive them; for they know not what they do" (Lk. 23:34). Jesus prays for those who have declared themselves his enemies. In the Beatitudes he taught, "Blessed are the merciful, for they shall obtain mercy" (Mt. 5:7); and in the Our Father he commanded us to pray, "Forgive us our trespasses *as we forgive* those who trespass against us."

"[T]oday you will be with me in paradise" (Lk. 23:43). In the "good thief" we have an image of the sacrament of reconciliation: With *contrition* he *confesses* his sin. He accepts his temporal punishment as the means to make *amends* for his crimes. As a result, Jesus *absolves* his sins.

"Behold your mother!" (Jn. 19:27). Mary gazes up at her Son as he redeems the world in the flesh he took from her. She knows that this is the moment for which Simeon sought to prepare her, "and a sword will pierce through your own soul also, that thoughts out of many hearts may be revealed" (Lk. 2:35). The Passion of the Son is the passion of the mother. She must reaffirm the "yes" she made at the Annunciation. With Jesus she prays, "Father, into your hands I commit my spirit" (Lk. 23:46).

Decade of the Rosary: Our Father, ten Hail Marys, Glory Be, Fatima Prayer

Pray: Dear Jesus, standing with your mother at the foot of your Cross and filled with your Spirit, we pray…

Chaplet Intercession: Father, give us the grace to forgive those who sin against us and those dear to us. Cause your mercy to triumph in our hearts and in the hearts of every person who has been victimized.

Decade of the Chaplet: "Eternal Father…," ten "For the sake…"

Triple Recitation of the Trisagion ("Holy God, Holy Mighty…"); *conclude with Hail Holy Queen*

The Burial of Christ, Titian, 1559

THE GLORIOUS MYSTERIES
GLORY STREAMS FROM THE CROSS

The Resurrection, Andrea Mantegna, 1457-1459

THE RESURRECTION

(JOHN 20:11-29)

Scripture tells us that Jesus's humanity was glorified in the Resurrection, *because he "became obedient unto death"* (Phil. 2:8). Our Lord's humanity was changed in the Resurrection – raised to a new, indestructible life (Heb. 7:16). And yet, Jesus retains his wounds. He shows them to the apostles as the proof of his identity. The wounds in his hands, feet, and side now adorn his humanity like priceless jewels, the eternal testimony to his love.

It is in the upper room that Jesus sends the Apostles forth to celebrate the sacrament of mercy. There, on that very first Easter, Jesus made provision for all of the times that we will fall. Jesus obtained mercy for us at the Cross, and it now flows to us through his pierced and glorified heart in the sacraments. As we read earlier in John's Gospel, "If any one thirst, let him come to me and drink. He who believes in me, as the Scripture has said, 'Out of his heart shall flow rivers of living water.' Now this [Jesus] said about the Spirit, which those who believed in him were to receive; *for as yet the Spirit had not been given, because Jesus was not yet glorified*" (Jn. 7:37-39).

Decade of the Rosary: Our Father, ten Hail Marys, Glory Be, Fatima Prayer

Pray: Dear Jesus, standing with your mother at the foot of your Cross and filled with your Spirit, we pray...

Chaplet Intercession: Father, give us the courage to make a thorough confession of our sins in the sacrament of reconciliation. Transform the "wounds" that sin has caused in our lives into well-springs of compassion for those with similar struggles.

Decade of the Chaplet: "Eternal Father...," ten "For the sake..."

The Incredulity of Saint Thomas, Caravaggio, 1601

The Ascension of Christ, Giotto di Bondone, 1305

THE ASCENSION

(ACTS 1:6-11)

Jesus ascends, as prophesied, into the cloud of God's glory (Dan. 7:13). He enters the true Temple, Heaven itself, to intercede on behalf of his Church. Jesus, who for a little while was made lower than the angels, is now crowned with glory and honor *because he suffered death* (Heb. 2:9). The song of the angels and saints reverberates throughout eternity: "By your blood [you] ransomed men for God from every tribe and tongue and people and nation. Worthy is the Lamb who was slain, to receive power and wealth and wisdom and might and honor and glory and blessing!" (Rev. 5:9, 12).

The victorious King, the Lion of the Tribe of Judah, stands before the Father's throne as a Lamb "who had been slain." He is our high priest, eternally making present his offering upon the Cross. He is filled with power and ready to breathe His Spirit upon the Church (Rev. 5:6). Through Jesus, *we* draw near to the Father's throne (Heb. 12:22-24). We, with the whole court of heaven, present our needs to the Father *through* Christ and his glorified wounds (Rev. 5:8; 8:4).

Decade of the Rosary: Our Father, ten Hail Marys, Glory Be, Fatima Prayer

Pray: Dear Jesus, standing with your mother at the foot of your Cross and filled with your Spirit, we pray...

Chaplet Intercession: Father, deepen our attention to you in prayer. Strip away our fears and distractions so that, united to Jesus, we may make a sincere offering of ourselves to you. Grace us to live out this offering in our actions.

Decade of the Chaplet: "Eternal Father...," ten "For the sake..."

Herz-Jesu-Darstellung, Gebhard Fugel, 1930

The Descent of the Holy Ghost,
Tiziano Vecellio (Titian), 1545

THE DESCENT OF
THE HOLY SPIRIT

(ACTS 2:1-24)

As Jesus entered upon his Passion, he told the apostles, "[I]f I do not go away, the Counselor will not come to you; but if I go, I will send him to you" (John 16:7). From heaven, Jesus breathes forth the Holy Spirit as a strong, driving wind upon his mother and the infant Church. The tongues of fire that appear above their heads witness to the fiery, purifying word they are sent to proclaim. They go forth, announcing the gospel of God's mercy to the pilgrims of Jerusalem.

Prior to the day of Pentecost the apostles and disciples knew the truth of Christ's teaching, but, seeing the suffering Jesus had endured, lacked the courage to proclaim the gospel to a hostile world. When the Spirit descended upon the Apostles, he did not make them impervious to suffering. Rather, he empowered them to embrace the Cross as the precondition of glory. "For [Jesus'] sake I have suffered the loss of all things... that I may know him and the power of his resurrection, and may share his sufferings, becoming like him in his death, that if possible I may attain the resurrection from the dead" (Phil. 3:8, 10-11).

Decade of the Rosary: Our Father, ten Hail Marys, Glory Be, Fatima Prayer

Pray: Dear Jesus, standing with your mother at the foot of your Cross and filled with your Spirit, we pray...

Chaplet Intercession: Father, empower us to overcome our fear of the Cross and boldly live Christ's life before the world. Stir up the gifts of the Spirit imparted to us in confirmation. Mother Mary, pray for us as you prayed for the infant Church.

Decade of the Chaplet: "Eternal Father...," ten "For the sake..."

Martyrdom of St. Peter, Caravaggio, 1600

Assumption of the Virgin, Titian, 1516–18

THE ASSUMPTION OF MARY

(REVELATION 11:19-12:2)

Mary, the woman who most intimately shared Jesus' life and Passion now shares his Resurrection and entrance into glory. Her body has been transformed and she is lifted up to his throne, clothed in the splendor of the Spirit, and presented to the Father.

This reality is not meant for Mary alone. She, like us, is a member of Christ's mystical body the Church. She shows us the splendor to which each of us is called. St. Paul wrote, "the Lord himself will descend from heaven with a cry of command…And the dead in Christ will rise first; then we who are alive, who are left, *shall be caught up together with them in the clouds to meet the Lord in the air*; and so we shall always be with the Lord" (1 Thess. 4:16-17). Christ's Passion has made this possible.

Decade of the Rosary: Our Father, ten Hail Marys, Glory Be, Fatima Prayer

Pray: Dear Jesus, standing with your mother at the foot of your Cross and filled with your Spirit, we pray…

Chaplet Intercession: Father, just as you took hold of Mary and lifted her up into the fullness of heavenly life, we pray that you will take hold of all who will die today. Purify them. Let the eyes of their souls gaze upon you in heaven, and the eyes of their body behold their savior in the resurrection.

Decade of the Chaplet: "Eternal Father…," ten "For the sake…"

Last Judgment, Leandro Bassano, 1595

The Coronation of the Virgin, Luca Signorelli, 1508

THE CORONATION OF MARY

(2 TIMOTHY 4:8)

One cannot meditate upon Mary's coronation for more than a moment without being struck by the contrast between her and the queens of this world. Mary was born into poverty, but with the nobility of a spotless soul. Instead of being instructed by senior courtiers, Mary worked side by side with the other women of her village. She knew the pain of a spouse considering divorce, the ache of widowhood, and the death of a child. And through it all she persisted in saying "yes" to God, "yes" to whatever he permitted. Instead of resting aloof in heavenly glory, she is a queen accessible to the most sinful and most scorned among us, wrapping her motherly arms around us and lifting us up in prayer to her Son. She really is a queen unlike any other; she has to be - she sits beside a king who was crowned with thorns.

At Mary's coronation she heard the words that each of us longs to hear, "Well done, good and faithful servant" (Mt. 25:23). We know that it was God's grace that brought Mary to such tremendous heights. He lavishes that grace upon us in the sacraments, our times of prayer, and in those moments when we act in accordance with his will. If we are faithful, we too will share Jesus' reign, "He who conquers, I will grant him to sit with me on my throne, as I myself conquered and sat down with my Father on his throne" (Rev. 3:21). Then our crowns of thorns will be transformed into crowns of glory.

Decade of the Rosary: Our Father, ten Hail Marys, Glory Be, Fatima Prayer

Pray: Dear Jesus, standing with your mother at the foot of your Cross and filled with your Spirit, we pray…

Chaplet Intercession: Most Holy Trinity, we ask for the grace to persevere in charity. Enflame our love of you and our neighbor that we may obtain the crowns you have prepared for us.

Decade of the Chaplet: "Eternal Father…," ten "For the sake…"

Triple Recitation of the Trisagion ("Holy God, Holy Mighty…"); conclude with Hail Holy Queen

Conclusion

I hope you have found this manner of prayer to be as fruitful as I have. In the Rosary we have gazed upon Jesus through the eyes and heart of his mother; and in the Chaplet, through Christ, we have petitioned the Father to pour out his mercy in the form of transformative graces. In our meditation we have seen the tree of death transformed into the tree of life – as well as how the roots of this tree extend all the way back to the first moments of Christ's incarnation. Our Catholic Faith is truly one organic whole! This only makes sense because our religion is not belief in a set of propositions, *but a relationship with the living God* (and the whole communion of saints brought to life in Him).

For relationships to flourish, they require time and attention. Personal, daily prayer is an absolute necessity for maintaining and deepening our union with the Most Holy Trinity. The Rosary and Chaplet are simple devotions to practice, but they take us into incredibly deep, life-giving spiritual waters. I believe that everyone has time in his or her schedule to heed the Blessed Mother's call to pray the Rosary daily – and I dare say, time to (at last occasionally) marry the Rosary to the Chaplet. Pray them in the car during your commute to work or school. Pray these prayers as you walk. (Download the audio files for this book, pop in your earbuds, and I will join you.) Let Mary ponder God's mysterious ways with you as she did on her way to visit Elizabeth. Allow Jesus to open the Scriptures for you as he did for the two disciples on the road to Emmaus. And call out, with the whole communion of saints, through Christ our high priest, for the mercy that we and our world so desperately need.

CPSIA information can be obtained
at www.ICGtesting.com
Printed in the USA
BVHW01*1405280218
509108BV00001B/1/P